*EXPLORATION INTO EXPERIENCE*

# THE MYSTERY OF CREATION

Brenda Lealman

and

Edward Robinson

CHRISTIAN EDUCATION MOVEMENT

ISBN 0 905022 83 1

We are grateful to the following for permission to use copyright material:

Mr Patrick Bailey; Öffentliche Kunstsammlung, Basle; Miss Dorothea Blom; Mr Dennis Hawkins; Mr Allen Hicks; Miss Charlotte Mayer; Mr David Neilson; Mr Hilary Robinson; Miss Alison Webb.

---

This series, *Exploration into Experience*, is being prepared by the Christian Education Movement in collaboration with the Religious Experience Research Unit, Manchester College, Oxford.

2

# INTRODUCTION

"In the beginning was the Word, and the Word was with God, and the Word was God."

So begins St John's Gospel. What does it mean? And is the meaning any less mysterious when we are told that what is here translated as 'Word' is that LOGOS which can also mean reason, order, design, purpose?

However we look at, however we try to comprehend it, creation is mysterious. Christians, following the old Hebraic tradition, say that God created the world, created the universe. But how is that to be understood?

Furthermore, if we believe this, there are other questions to be faced; for if we think of God as both good and all-powerful, how is it that there is so much in His creation that seems so evil? And does that creation really appear to be ordered and purposive? Much of the time it looks to be in the control of forces that are random and undirected to any end.

These questions have been endlessly debated. They always will be. It is not the purpose of this book to make any contribution to that debate. Rather, what we offer here are some reflections on the mystery of creation itself.

Here, then, we shall be drawing on the Bible, and in particular on the poetry of the Old Testament, to show how a particular people understood creation and how they recorded their response to it. Alongside these insights we also give examples of how some artists and photographers of our own time have expressed their response to creation and shared in the creative processes. That, however, is not all.

It may often be valuable to note the ways in which others have explored these mysteries but we ourselves need to be challenged to some creative exploration of our own. So if sometimes there does not seem to be any obvious connection between the pictures on the pages which follow and the quotations that accompany them, then, perhaps we must stretch our imagination further. It is up to our own creativity to make the connections, to discover them; perhaps even sometimes to invent them for ourselves.

It is, after all, the exploration of our own experience that this series is concerned with. So what do we ourselves make of these words and images? 'Make something of' our experience is indeed what life is all about. To this extent we too are, all of us, involved in creation.

In learning to do this we may in some small way learn to look with more imagination, and so with more open and grateful eyes, on the mystery of creation.

The earth was without form and void, and darkness was upon the face of the deep; and the Spirit of God was moving over the face of the waters.

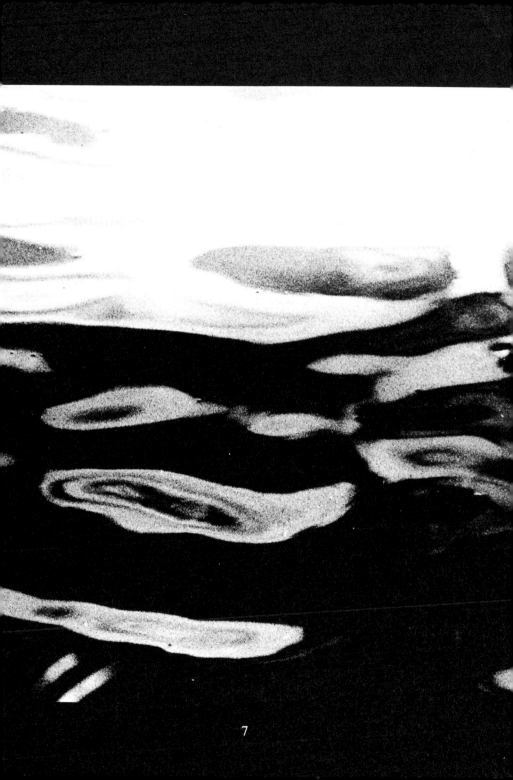

Of old thou didst lay the foundation of
    the earth,
  and the heavens are the work of thy
    hands.

They will perish, but thou dost
    endure;
  they will all wear out like a
    garment.

Thou changest them like raiment, and
    they pass away;
  but thou art the same, and thy years
    have no end.

That which is, is far off, and deep,
very deep;
Who can find it out?

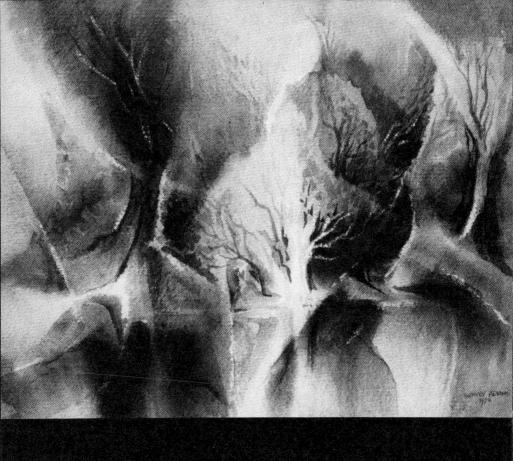

# SEEING

What do we see as we look around at the creation?

A rich landscape of mysterious and immense horizons and possibilities? Or, a wasteland? Just "a heap of broken images, where the sun beats, and the dead tree gives no shelter?"

Meaninglessness? The futility, the emptiness referred to by the writer of Ecclesiastes? Or do we feel that our attempts to control, to explain, to make sense are sufficient?

To many people it seems that with the advance of scientific knowledge the universe is becoming less and less mysterious. The area of what cannot be accounted for or predicted becomes smaller and smaller. The whole of life will surely in the end be explained in terms of cause and effect, in terms of natural forces interacting as chance alone dictates. The idea of a creative, purposive mind at work behind or within it becomes increasingly unnecessary. Perhaps it was only scientific ignorance in the first place that led us to believe that there must be some unknown force behind it all. The universe as a whole appears to leave no room for meaning or purpose. What was once thought of as 'the God of the gaps', the God who was brought in to explain the hitherto unexplainable, has become squeezed out: there is no need for him.

Nevertheless, something persists in us that asks questions of life; something that prevents us from finally accepting the idea that all existence is meaningless.

When we put these questions to life in general, Life with a capital L, there does seem to be no possibility of an answer. But when we think in terms of our own individual lives we find more reason to hope. We find something that can give them meaning, something that suggests a sense of direction. This causes trouble.

It causes trouble because in the universe as a whole we can find no evidence for such a direction. Pattern, yes; science has shown us how closely all the phenomena of the natural world are inter-related. Everywhere, more and more, we can see predictable regularities. But direction? It was once possible for men and women to believe in something they called 'progress'; as though the natural processes of evolution, as revealed by science, were all somehow combining to move towards the emergence of a better, more harmonious world.

Science in fact shows us no such thing. What we learn from it is that the seemingly tranquil 'balance of nature' is really a precarious equilibrium of mutually competitive and destructive forces.

Then again, when we employ the methods of science in the study of our own human nature we may learn much about the forces, social or psychological, that influence and often determine our behaviour, but little that will help towards that change of heart that the world so desperately needs if our species is to survive. The way things are going now, the only end to which we are making progress is the end of self-destruction.

So when we talk about the mystery of creation perhaps it is in our own selves that we should look for an understanding of it; in ourselves and in the inescapable need we feel to make something of our lives. Can it be that the mystery we perceive in creation is really only a reflection of the mystery of our own creativeness?

What then are the roots of this creativity of ours? And how is it that each one of us experiences it?

Each one of us? Not so, many people would say. Of course we know what sort of people are creative: writers, composers, painters, architects and the like. They are somehow different, or so we think. You need a touch of genius, the artistic temperament and so forth, to be creative.

Nothing of the sort. Consider Christ's story of the man who thought he was nothing special, the parable of the talents. This was addressed not to the man who had five talents or to the man who had three, but to the man with one; the man who thought so little of himself that he had better not take risks with the single gift he had.

Let us go back to those poets and artists, men and women whom we all recognize as creative. Gifted, we call them, and rightly so: creativity is a gift, but one that is given to all of us.

It is the gift of seeing new possibilities in things, new possibilities in people. To create means to realize these possibilities, to bring them into existence.

A gift, though, is not properly speaking a gift until it is received. So an essential part of being creative means being ready to recognize gifts, our own and those of others; to recognize them and to be grateful for them.

The truly creative person is the one who has come to accept the whole of life as a gift.

Nothing of this, however, would be possible if we as a species were not endowed with one all-important faculty.

Consider this question: what is it that makes our species different from other animals? Here is one answer. We alone have imagination. We alone can conceive of things being different from the way they are. We alone can dream of new possibilities, can set about realizing them. We alone can be creative.

To possess imagination gives us the key to another world: the world of the spirit. To this flight of the creative imagination there is no limit: no limit to the infinite possibilities we may open ourselves up to.

And it is in this opening-up that we make the great discovery: we are not probing emptiness. The reality we meet is not indifferent to our search. We encounter another and greater creativity; this is a two-way affair. There is a positive, more mysterious resonance, not just the echo of our own cry. We find that cry to be part of a reality greater than ourselves.

It is imagination, then, which can transform our experience, stretching perception into vision, a vision which leads to new perspectives, new ways of seeing. It is the creative imagination which can rescue us from the meaninglessness which continually threatens us.

Without this creative openness which we call imagination there would simply never be those moments of affirmation when new horizons of reality reveal themselves to us, when we see, as Tennyson puts it, that:

> All experience is an arch where thro'
> Gleams that untravell'd world whose margin fades
> For ever and for ever when I move.

Whither shall I go from thy Spirit?
  Or whither shall I flee from thy
    presence?

If I take the wings of the morning
    and dwell in the uttermost parts of
      the sea,
Even there thy hand shall lead me,
    and thy right hand shall hold me.

If I say, "Let only darkness cover me,
    and the light about me be night",
Even the darkness is not dark to thee,
    the night is bright as the day;
    for darkness is as light with thee.

23

Behold, we know not anything;
I can but trust that good shall fall
At last – far off – at last, to all,
And every winter change to spring.

So runs my dream: but what am I?
An infant crying in the night:
An infant crying for the light:
And with no language but a cry.

I, wisdom, dwell in prudence,
and I find knowledge and
discretion.

The Lord created me at the beginning
of his work,
the first of his acts of old.

Ages ago I was set up,
at the first, before the beginning of
the earth.

When there were no depths I was
brought forth,
when there were no springs
abounding with water.

Before the mountains had been
shaped,
before the hills, I was brought forth;

Before he had made the earth with its
fields,
or the first dust of the world.

When he established the heavens, I
was there,
when he drew a circle on the face of
the deep,

When he assigned to the sea its limit,
so that the waters might not
transgress his command.

When he marked out the foundations
   of the earth,
   then I was beside him, like a master
   workman;

And I was daily his delight
   rejoicing before him always,

Rejoicing in his inhabited world
   and delighting in the sons of men.

# SHAPING

The Bible is about creation.

We may sometimes think of creation as the way everything began, as though the universe must have had a beginning and the account at the opening of Genesis provides answers to questions about how this happened. Or we may think about creation as a kind of magic, the sort of supernatural power encountered in fairy stories by which coaches are made out of pumpkins, frogs are turned into princes, feasts and treasures conjured out of thin air.

Either way is to miss the heart of the matter.

Creation means giving shape and meaning to what was previously, as Genesis says, "without form and void".

Out of a vast watery waste, the heavens and earth were formed. Out of dust, man was shaped. The great God "kneeled down in the dust toiling over the lump of clay" until he shaped "a living being", both of dust and of spirit; flesh and spirit in a single mysterious being – that free spirit which is expressed through the creative imagination: a creature to whom was given the ability to share in the process of creation.

There was literally no limit to the variety of forms which that process might take. The poets and prophets, historians and story-tellers of the Old Testament experienced creation as an on-going sense of the presence and activity in their lives of that shaping, purposive force which we first meet in Genesis. So Jeremiah describes how in the potter's house the word of the Lord came to him:

O house of Israel, can I not do with you as this potter has done?

Behold the clay in the potter's hand, so are you in my hand.

Expression was given to this sense in terms sometimes of wonder, fear and obedience, at other times with resistance and even anger.

Again, the people of the Old Testament, the Jews, believed that they themselves, as part of the creative process, had been given a special gift: the gift of being able, more than any other people, to respond to that creative force. They were, in this sense, God's chosen people. This gave them a special place in history, and also a special responsibility – to be themselves creative in their response to the creation. The Old Testament is the story of that response, sometimes gloriously creative, sometimes humiliating in its failure.

The Old Testament is therefore in a double sense a record of creation. It tells of the creation of the natural world, and of man as part of that world, by God, and of God's creative purpose working itself out in human history.

It also tells of one people's awareness of the part they felt called on to play in that creative pattern, a pattern which, but for them, might never come to completion.

So throughout the Bible we continually find records of experiences which inspired men and women to see new possibilities in creation. We find visions and images through which they expressed their yearning for what might be, their celebration of what creation is and might become. There are pictures of men beating swords into ploughshares and spears into pruning hooks; of dry bones being filled with new life; of the poor and disabled shuffling into the Messianic feast.

Images of this kind, of course, are not confined to the Bible; they occur in every religious tradition. Our own is particularly rich in them as is natural in a religion which gives so important a place to the material world; and this richness is reflected in our western culture today. There is thus a real continuity from the symbolic stories of the Old Testament and the parables of the New to the kind of imaginative exploration of man's place in the universe which we find, for example, in the more searching forms of contemporary science fiction.

Thou didst set the earth on its
    foundations,
    so that it should never be shaken.

Thou didst cover it with the deep as
    with a garment;
    the waters stood above the
    mountains.

O Lord, how manifold are thy works!
    In wisdom hast thou made them all;
    the earth is full of thy creatures.

Yonder is the sea, great and wide,
    which teems with things
    innumerable,
    living things both small and great.

When thou hidest thy face, they are
    dismayed;
    when thou takest away their breath,
    they die
    and return to their dust.

When thou sendest forth thy Spirit,
    they are created;
    and thou renewest the face of the
    ground.

God creates the birds of the air & the fish of the sea.

Fifth day of Creation: Genesis. Dorothea 1976

Lord, all my longing is known to thee,
my sighing is not hidden from thee.

My heart throbs, my strength fails me;
and the light of my eyes – it also has
gone from me.

I am like a deaf man, I do not hear,
like a dumb man who does not open
his mouth.

But for thee, O Lord, do I wait;
it is thou, O Lord my God, who wilt
answer.

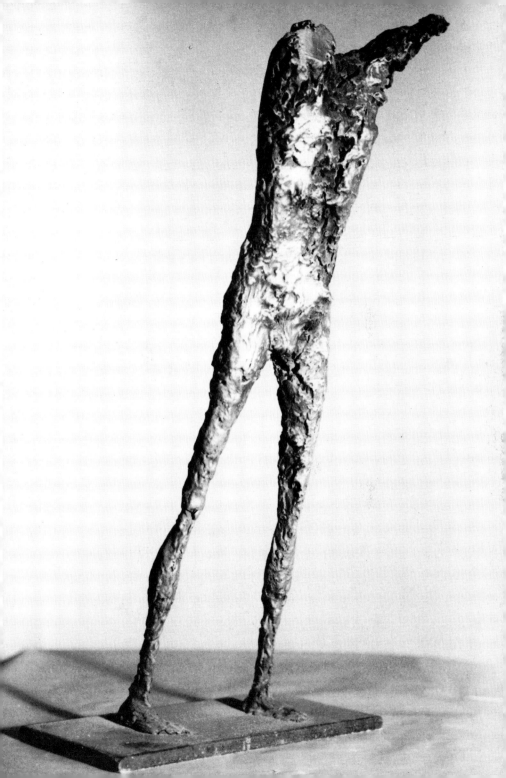

O Lord what is man that thou dost
    regard him,
  or the son of man that thou dost
    think of him?

Man is like a breath,
  his days are like a passing shadow.

Man puts his hand to the flinty rock,
   and overturns mountains by the
   roots.

He cuts out channels in the rocks,
   and his eye sees every precious
   thing.

He binds up the streams so that they
   do not trickle,
   and the thing that is hid he brings
   forth to light.

But where shall wisdom be found?
   And where is the place of
   understanding?

Man does not know the way to it,
   and it is not found in the land of the
   living.

In parts of our cities we're like men in the desert, in a cement desert; there are no trees, no flowers. But we can still somehow manage to make gardens. So I pick up all this technological junk and I make little gardens, little chapels, little shrines with it. I think man is that kind of creature. Even if he's put in the most horrible spot he'll continue trying to make a beautiful place he can say prayers in.

You know how it is; you go in the rain along a dark street and the street lights are shining – it's such beautiful poetry. I've always wanted to paint that and I never could. It's like this with this box: you move into some mysterious universe, the lights shine, and you feel you are approaching something very special, very mysterious.

The more we go into the mystery the more we seem to be entering a kind of rich darkness. It's a good darkness. It's to do with silence.

Before the mountains were brought
    forth,
or ever thou had'st formed the earth
    and the world,
from everlasting to everlasting thou
    art God.

# TRANSCENDING

The wind blows where it wills, and
you hear the sound of it, but you do
not know whence it comes or whither
it goes; so it is with every one that is
born of the Spirit.

We yearn for what we cannot achieve. The Bible is full of expressions of this yearning. Abraham left his home and people in search of a destiny, an unknown land, a blessing beyond his vision; Moses longed for freedom and justice for his people; Jeremiah for his countrymen to see that religion is not outward observance and ritual but an inner response to God; Paul for love instead of rules.

We are always dreaming dreams, seeing new possibilities. Imagination gets to work and gives them shape. We plunge into creation without knowing exactly what the end is to be. But behind the shaping, within the creating the vision grows – vision of something always further on, still further in. Something still unachieved, still to come. In Browning's well-known words:

Ah, but a man's reach should exceed his grasp
Or what's a heaven for?

In our relationship with our fellow men and women too this sense of the 'if only' is the mainspring of all responsible action, all pastoral caring, all social idealism, all political commitment.

Then there is the vision of the poet and the artist.

Every true work of art points beyond itself, often beyond what the artist himself or herself is conscious of having expressed, so that we too, all of us, not only can but must respond in our own ways to that vision if its full meaning is to be made known.

Even the humblest work of art is a reminder that we must always be ready to go on beyond what we know of ourselves.

Every religious tradition, however, has recognized that there are times in the spiritual life when all images must be left behind; times when imagination can only be a distraction.

At such times all that either language or images can do is to point beyond themselves.

The last step of reason, said Pascal, is to recognize that there are many things that lie beyond it. The imagination, too, will in the end discover that it can only bring us so far and no further: to a region where all images must be left behind.

We end, therefore, with three writers who came to recognize this impasse and gave expression to it each in his own way.

The first is the unknown author of the fourteenth century treatise on the spiritual life, *The Cloud of Unknowing*.

The second is the twentieth century painter Kasimir Malevich, for whom the white square came eventually to symbolize a world beyond objects.

The third is the author of the book of Job, who in direct confrontation with God was thrust beyond his wildest imagining by the transfiguring terror of what he saw, and was reduced to silence.

The higher part of contemplation, at least as we know it in this life, is wholly caught up in darkness, and in this cloud of unknowing, with an outreaching love and a blind groping for the naked being of God, Himself and Him only.

Therefore the vigorous working of your imagination, which is always so active when you set yourself to this blind contemplation, must as often be suppressed.

I have torn through the blue
lampshade of colour and come out
into the white. Sail out after me,
fellow aviators, into the chasm; the
free, white chasm of infinity is before
us.

Then Job answered the Lord:
"Behold I am of small account; what
shall I answer thee?
I lay my hand upon my mouth.

I have spoken once, and I will not
answer;
Twice, but I will proceed no
further."

## Notes on the Text

p. 6.   Genesis 1:2.
p. 8.   Psalm 102:25ff.
p. 10.  Ecclesiastes 7:24.
p. 14.  "A heap of broken images . . ." T. S. Eliot, *The Waste Land.*
p. 20.  "All experience is an arch . . ." Tennyson, *Ulysses.*
p. 22.  Psalm 139:7ff.
p. 24.  Tennyson, *In Memoriam.*
p. 26.  Proverbs 8:12ff.
p. 28.  Proverbs 8:25ff.
p. 30.  Proverbs 8:29ff.
p. 34.  ". . . kneeled down in the dust . . ." James Wheldon Johnson, *The Creation.*
p. 35.  Jeremiah 18:6.
p. 38.  Psalm 104:5ff.
p. 40.  Psalm 38:9ff.
p. 42.  Psalm 144:3f.
p. 44.  Job 28:9ff.
p. 46.  Alba Taylor, in interview (unpublished) with Edward Robinson.
p. 48.  Psalm 90:2.
p. 52.  John 3:8.
p. 53.  "Ah, but a man's reach . . ." Browning, *Andrea Del Sarto.*
p. 56.  *The Cloud of Unknowing*, ed. C. Wolters (Penguin, London, 1961) pp. 64f.
p. 58.  Kasimir Malevich, *Non-Objective Creation and Suprematism*: Catalogue of the Tenth State Exhibition; Moscow 1919.
p. 60.  Job 40:3–5.

# Notes on the Illustrations

p. 7.   Allen Hicks, photograph; *Murrumbidgee River*, Australia.
p. 9.   Allen Hicks, photograph; *Rocks*.
p. 11.  Alison Webb, photograph; *Through the Trees*.
p. 12.  Hervey Adams, *The Mystery of Growth*; watercolour.
p. 21.  Dennis Hawkins, *Horizons*; black and white emulsion painting.
p. 23.  Otto Freundlich, *Composition, 1932*; oil. Ôffentliche Kunstsammlung, Basle.
p. 25.  Allen Hicks, photograph; *Murrumbidgee River*.
p. 27.  Denis Mitchell, *St Merryn*; bronze. (Photograph: Hilary Robinson).
p. 29.  Charlotte Mayer, *Spiral Form*; bronze. (Photograph: Peter Keen).
p. 31.  Edward Robinson, photograph; *Tumbuka Girls, Zambia*.
p. 32.  Michelangelo, *Prisoner Awakening*; marble. Galleria dell Accademia, Florence.
p. 39.  Dorothea Blom, *Creation Continues*; watercolour.
p. 41.  Charlotte Mayer, *Man*; resin bronze. (Photograph: Stella Samuel).
p. 43.  David Neilson, photograph; *Glasgow*.
p. 45.  David Neilson, photograph; *The Breaker's Yard*.
p. 47.  Alba Taylor, *Triptych: Meditation*; mixed media. (Photograph: Hilary Robinson).
p. 49.  Patrick Bailey, photograph; *Callanish*.
p. 50.  Brian Donnan, photograph; *Reaching Out*.

By the same authors:

EXPLORATION INTO EXPERIENCE: I

# THE IMAGE OF LIFE

*Very impressive . . . a most imaginative approach which will appeal to the younger generation . . . A most beautiful production which one can meditate with great joy.*

The Bishop of Winchester

*It seems to be one of those pioneering studies that are quoted for decades after. Many congratulations.*

Alastair Smart, Professor
of Fine Art, Nottingham

*It has opened the door to a whole new world of possibilities for me. We use so many words in the church . . . It is exciting to think of trying to communicate the Gospel in other ways.*

TV Producer

EXPLORATION INTO EXPERIENCE: II

# KNOWING & UNKNOWING

*We still see through a glass darkly in spite of our growth in knowledge of human behaviour. This book should be a welcome addition to the collection of anyone who likes to use his or her eyes and mind in the cause of making that glass a little less obscure.*

Faith and Freedom

*A really exciting series. We live in times when the young are hungry to find deep ways of understanding and purpose, and the visual route is one they may more easily take. This is an aspect of RE which is very much worth following up, and we are indebted to the authors for the pioneer work in which they are engaged.*

AVA Resources Review

*Printed by The Leagrave Press Ltd, Luton and London*